SPECTACULAR SHETLAND

DISCOVER BRITAIN

Spectacular Shetland

by
Robert Plant

Illustrated by Grace Plant

JOHN RITCHIE LTD
CHRISTIAN PUBLICATIONS
40 Beansburn, Kilmarnock, Scotland

ISBN-13: 978 1 910513 17 0

www.ritchiechristianmedia.co.uk

Typeset by John Ritchie Ltd., Kilmarnock
Printed by Bell & Bain, Glasgow

Contents

Introduction

Spectacular Shetland is the first in a series of books written especially for the younger generation who want to know more about both Great Britain and their Great Bible. It is intended that the Discover Britain series will eventually build into an exciting library of several titles. The fascinating stories are told by looking back at history or by surveying landscapes and getting close to wildlife. The writer intends the books not only to be educational but also spiritual as he points his readers to vitally important truths from the Bible, God's Word. So children, pack your cases, fasten your seat belts and get ready to go on a voyage of discovery across the exciting and interesting countries and islands that make up Great Britain.

Discover Shetland

Remote and desolate, magnificent and mysterious, Shetland is the most northerly part of the British Isles, lying over one hundred miles north of the coast of mainland Scotland. It is made up of more than one hundred separate islands, from tiny outcrops of rock jutting out of the sea to major landmasses such as the main island, called Mainland, yet only seventeen of these islands are inhabited by people. From Unst in the north to Fair Isle in the south the islands stretch in length for over one hundred miles, and spread for fifty miles from east to west.

The majority of the roads which cross the islands are single track, having wider areas provided every three or four hundred metres to allow cars to pass one another. These roads are usually incredibly windy as they twist and turn around hills and the numerous sea lochs that dominate so much of this wild and rugged land. Despite the large size of the area which these islands cover, they are inhabited by around only twenty-three thousand people, which means that often you can travel for miles on some of the more remote roads without encountering another car! Walking is a wonderful way to explore the islands' breathtaking beauty and diverse wildlife, but again don't be too surprised if you find that you are the only person on the footpath! This is a great place to enjoy peace and tranquillity as you ponder the amazing wonders and diversity of God's creation.

It's an interesting fact that the capital, Lerwick, is actually closer to the Arctic than to London, so if you visit be sure to take warm clothes, as even in the height of summer Shetland can be a chilly place! Due to their remoteness and cooler climate, these islands host a wealth of wildlife that you are unlikely to see in other parts of the British Isles. Look out to sea from the cliffs around the main island's most southerly point, Sumburgh Head, an RSPB (Royal Society for the Protection of Birds) reserve, and you may be fortunate enough to spot orcas (killer whales), minke whales or the occasional dolphin as they come close to the shore seeking food among the great shoals of fish that feed in the plankton-rich waters. Head via ferry to the most northerly islands of Unst and Yell and you might catch a glimpse of one of Britain's rarest and most beautiful birds, the red-necked phalarope, which is found in these more northern extremities of Shetland. A must for any serious wildlife enthusiast visiting these interesting islands are the playful otters as they swim and frolic in the many lochs that dissect the islands. These wonderful creatures, which normally live in fresh water, have adapted to sea life and can often be spotted as they run along the shoreline in search of both food and adventure. Most of the wildlife that is commonly seen around the seas, cliffs and lochs has been given local Shetland names which we hope to learn as we look more closely at some of their behaviour and habitats.

You only have to travel a couple of miles to be aware that Shetland is surrounded by water. In fact, not so much surrounded by water, but totally dominated by it! The sea is everywhere, with tidal bays, sea inlets and small voes running often a few miles inland through the rocky valleys that have been carved by the sea's incessant pounding and power over many years. A voe is a closed tidal waterway leading inland from the sea, and the word 'voe' occurs regularly throughout Shetland, from the large oil terminal at Sullom Voe in the North Mainland, to the village of Burravoe in Yell. There's the small hamlet of Selivoe in the west and the settlement of Voe itself, about twenty miles north of Lerwick. Other smaller voes are Aith Voe, Dury Voe and Swining Voe, to name but a few. There are around twenty-five voes that cut through and across these wonderful islands, bringing a beauty and uniqueness to this area that is hard to find anywhere else in the world.

Another word that you will soon become familiar with in Shetland is 'sound'! A sound is a stretch of water that runs between two islands; for instance, you have Yell Sound that runs between the North Mainland and the island of Yell, and Bluemull Sound that crosses between Yell and Unst. Further south, there is Mousa Sound, separating the island of Mousa from the South Mainland. In addition, there are the villages of Baltasound and Uyeasound in Unst and the area of Sound itself, just south of Lerwick.

Lerwick is the name of the capital town which comes from the old Norse name, Leirvik, which means 'muddy bay'. If, however, you are looking for lots of shops in which to indulge yourself with the latest fashions or new electronic game you may well be disappointed. The large fashion chains found in other towns throughout the United Kingdom are missing from Lerwick, giving the town an almost Victorian and antiquated feel. If you want the latest accessories you will need to shop by mail order from mainland Britain! What you do get in Lerwick, though, is the ferry that runs to Aberdeen, lying some two hundred and ten miles south; Kirkwall, the capital of Orkney, which is situated around one hundred and thirty miles south; and the Faroe Isles that lie around another two hundred and thirty miles north-west of Shetland, out in the Atlantic Ocean. So this is the wonderful place that we hope to explore in our Shetland Adventure, the land of voes and Vikings, wind and wildlife, sea and sky. This is Shetland!

Super Seals

Common Seal

It would be hard to visit Shetland without at some stage catching sight of one of the two species of seals which inhabit these islands all year round. Shetland hosts both common and grey seals, which number about four thousand in total. This means that the Shetlands have nearly a quarter of all the seal population in the United Kingdom. Locally, seals are known as 'selkies'. The two species are not easy to recognise without seeing their faces. The common seal has a more dog-like face, curving up from its eyes, whereas the grey seal's face is more rectangular and runs in a straight line from its nose to the top of its head like the head of a horse, explaining why it often carries the name of 'horsehead seal'!

Up until only a few decades ago both seals were hunted for their fur, sometimes with over one thousand seal pups (baby seals) being killed each year. Good news for seals arrived in 1973 in the way of laws to ban the hunting of common seals in Shetland. Sadly, such protection for the grey seal did not come into force until the mid 1980s when they too finally received protected status! How different is this to God's wonderful message of salvation, where all who are in need can find salvation in the person of God's Son, the Lord Jesus Christ. The Bible says, *"For God so loved the world, that He gave His only begotten Son, that whosoever believeth in Him should not perish, but have everlasting life"* (John ch3v16). God's love is not exclusive, selecting some but rejecting others; it includes everyone, allowing each to decide for him or herself whether to repent of their sins and take the Lord Jesus as their Saviour. For those who do trust the Lord Jesus, God promises His daily help, strength and presence, as He says, *"I will never leave thee, nor forsake thee"* (Hebrews ch13v5).

The grey seal is generally larger than the common seal, with the bulls (male seals) measuring around two and a half to three metres in length and weighing up to 300kg! The cows (female seals) are much smaller, usually only reaching a maximum length of around two metres and weighing in at a more respectable 150 to 200kg. The two varieties of seals have very different life cycles to each other, with grey seals having their pups in October, usually on some of the most barren and inaccessible beaches on the islands. The pups grow quickly, their diet consisting of the very rich milk provided by their mothers which contains over fifty percent fat! No worries about obesity with grey seals then! When the seal is three weeks old it will be able to feed on what will eventually be its staple diet - fish. By this time the baby seal will have added anything between 20kg and 40kg in weight just by drinking its mother's milk! At one month old it will be able to go for its first hunting and swimming lesson in the deep waters around the islands' coasts.

The common seal in Shetland (often also called the harbour seal) is recognised as being of great international importance. Many, including the author, believe these seals to be a much friendlier-looking variety than the grey seals. The common seals are smaller than the grey, usually not growing beyond two metres in length and weighing no more than about 130kg. Interestingly, the female can outlive the male by up to ten years, with some often being recorded at around thirty-five years old. It is commonly assumed that this age discrepancy is caused as the result of the strains placed upon the males during the mating and breeding seasons when they often have to fight other males in order to mate with suitable females! It is estimated that there are around half a million common seals in the world and each one has a unique pattern of spots upon their bodies with no two being alike. Amazingly, common seals have been recorded swimming to depths of 450m in search of food and can hold their breath for up to ten minutes; however, three minute dives are more the norm. The common seal pups are usually born in June, the parent seeking out some of the more sheltered bays and voes for the birth. Although able to swim almost from birth, the baby seals will be weaned by their mothers for around six weeks before being ready to hunt fish for themselves. Look out for seals in just about any of the voes that cut into the islands from the great ocean that surrounds them.

Clown of the Seas

Whenever you see a puffin there is something about it that just makes you want to smile! They look comical, walk in an odd manner and even fly in the most ungainly way imaginable. Welcome to the chapter about the clown of all birds - the puffin, or 'tammie norie' to the Shetland islander.

Puffin

The puffin is actually a type of auk. Other auks you may come across in the Shetlands include both the beautifully streamlined guillemots and the razorbills with their rather odd-looking beaks. There are three types of puffin in the world: one is the tufted puffin, which has a smaller beak and two bright yellow tufts on either side of its head. Another is the horned puffin, part of whose beak resembles a curved horn. These are only found in the North Pacific Ocean so you are highly unlikely to find one here! However, you should most certainly see the third type, the much more common Atlantic puffin, and you will be able to see it up close and personal too.

Perhaps the best place to observe these most entertaining birds is at the RSPB site around the Sumburgh Head lighthouse at the southernmost tip of the mainland. Here you will be able to get almost within an arm's length of these wonderful, brightly-billed, quizzical birds. However, if you are prepared to travel a little further north to the Icelandic owned Westmann Isles (and, after all, the Shetland Islands are halfway there from the British mainland) you may see colonies estimated at between one and four million! Don't forget to listen for the extraordinary sound of them 'talking' to each other. It's a sound that you will remember for a long time to come! Watch for long enough and you may be fortunate enough to see a pair clashing their bills (beaks) together, almost like a medieval sword fighter, as they try to keep them clean, sharp and healthy for both digging their burrows and catching fish.

This behaviour is also used to re-establish the bond between pairs that have been separated at sea during the winter months. Many seabirds mate for life, even returning to the same burrow year after year in order to lay their eggs and raise their young, and most puffins are no different.

The comical-looking, multi-coloured beak that we all love so much loses its colour (these colours are actually plates that drop off) during the puffin's winter days at sea, the bright colours only returning in spring when the puffin heads for land in order to find its mate and commence breeding.

The beautiful, almost rainbow-coloured beak of the 'clown of the seas' reminds me of the time when God first placed some of those magnificent colours in the sky in the form of a rainbow. This was given to Noah as a promise following the great flood that destroyed every living creature upon the face of the earth (except Noah and those in the ark with him) because of their rebellion against God. You can read about this in the Bible in Genesis chapter 9, verses 13 to 16. The Bible also says of God that *"He is faithful that promised"* (Hebrews ch10v23). This means that when God promises something He will always faithfully keep that promise. So, just as God has never flooded the whole world again, we can be sure that He will keep any promises that He makes and that He is worthy of our trust. To those who have trusted Him as Saviour, the Lord Jesus promises, *"Lo, I am with you alway, even unto the end of the world"* (Matthew ch28v20). Now that's a promise from God worth having!

The short, powerful wings were not only created to allow the puffin to fly through the air but underwater as well! Wow, what a wonderful design feature that is! When flying, the puffin must beat its wings around four hundred times a minute in order to keep airborne! That's about six or seven beats per second. Once it arrives at its destination it then often has to swim under water in order to catch fish. This is a super-fit bird!

At breeding time the female lays a single egg and both parents take it in turn to incubate it (keep it warm) by holding it close to their bodies with their wings. Once it has hatched, the chick is fed by both birds until it is old enough to fly. When it fledges and leaves the nest it will spend possibly the first four or five years of its life out at sea before returning to shore in order to breed.

The puffin is well known for its wonderful fishing ability, being able to catch and hold up to twenty small fish (often sandeels) crossways in its beak all at the same time - a truly remarkable feat! This allows it to spend more time fishing and less time feeding its young as they can bring several fish back from their trips rather than just feeding the chick with one fish at a time.

Sadly, this beautiful bird is not exempt from people hunting it, and even today puffins are caught and killed in both Iceland and the Faroe Islands for their eggs, feathers and meat. In Iceland, puffin turns up on many a restaurant menu and puffin hearts are considered a local delicacy.

Let There Be Lights

Have you ever fancied visiting a lighthouse to see how it works? Imagine looking at the great, powerful lamp that is able to be seen many miles out at sea. The giant glass reflector, almost like a huge mirror, is very impressive as it spins around in front of the lamp, giving every lighthouse in the world a different sequence of flashes so that they can be identified by passing ships. Look at how it almost seems to float around the lamp, without friction, due to its beautifully oiled runners. Yes, lighthouses are impressive buildings, not only for their often dramatic positions, but also for the amazing engineering that makes them work so wonderfully.

Muckle Flugga Lighthouse

Well, if you visit Shetland there are three lighthouses where you can actually stay in the keeper's cottage! These are found in Sumburgh in the south, Eshaness on the wild and dramatic north coast cliffs, and on the island of Bressay on the entrance to Lerwick harbour. Oh, just one thing, you are not allowed to turn out the light at night!

Shetland boasts around thirty-nine lighthouses, perhaps more than any other group of islands in the world! A large number of these are in the north, running through Yell Sound and Sullom Voe in order to bring safety and protection to the many oil tankers that daily use that passage of water. Lighthouses can also be found on Fair Isle, which lies some twenty-four miles to the south of the main islands, and on the Out Skerries islands, the furthest east you can go in Shetland. The one here is perhaps one of Shetland's most beautiful lighthouses, rising high, tall and straight, like a giant white finger pointing towards the sky.

All lighthouses across the world have the same vitally important job to do - to warn ships of the approaching dangers of land and rocks should they stray too close. Most of Britain's lighthouses were erected during the Victorian era to try and stop the appalling loss of life that was taking place among sailors and fishermen as they ran aground on dangerous rocks and projecting landmasses around Britain's coasts. This was no different in Shetland, so in order to help save lives and protect shipping, the first lighthouse was built at Sumburgh Head in 1821, designed by Robert Stevenson Snr; this was to be the first of many built by him and his family. The last to be built was on the island of Foula to the West in 1986. The Ve Skerries lighthouse was built in 1979 on a group of rocks that have claimed several ships, including two that we will read of later in this book. There are also many other smaller warning lights and navigational markers helping to protect the major shipping lanes around the islands.

Shetland boasts the most northerly lighthouse in the British Isles with the oddly named Muckle Flugga lighthouse which stands some distance offshore from the coast of Unst. Its position on top of a steep sided outcrop of rock is dramatic indeed and well worth the effort to view. Let's be honest, how many folk can claim to have stood at the northern end of Great Britain? Interestingly, Muckle Flugga lighthouse was designed by Thomas Stevenson, the father of Robert Louis Stevenson who wrote the great book entitled 'Treasure Island'.

Each lighthouse you see will warn of danger to passing ships but also often give a welcome sight of land to sailors who may have been at sea for many days. How welcoming such a beam of light must be, especially when they are able to confirm their location by the sequence of light flashes each lighthouse produces. In the Bible the Lord Jesus twice said that He was *"the light of the world"* (John ch8v12 and ch9v5), providing protection and safety from the jagged rocks of sin that threaten to wreck and ruin our lives. He promises to those who trust Him as Saviour and follow His light, *"He that followeth Me shall not walk in darkness, but shall have the light of life"* (John ch8v12).

All the lighthouses in Shetland are now fully automated, which means that they no longer require a lighthouse keeper to ensure that they are lit and stay on through the night.

Playful Fisher of the Sea

Stay perfectly still by the water's edge, especially at low tide, and you might just spot one of Britain's most interesting, but often elusive, animals - the otter, or 'dratsie' to the Shetlander. These beautiful creatures will bring a pleasure that is hard to match when you do finally manage to catch a glimpse of one as it runs to and fro among the kelp beds that are exposed at low tide, using its sensitive whiskers to try and seek out food among the seaweed. The otter is a close relative of the weasel, the polecat and, oddly enough, the badger.

Otter

The Shetland otters number about one thousand and are now thankfully a protected species, although sadly this was not always the case. Otter fur was considered a real speciality among fashion designers and a good pelt (skin) could fetch a high price when sold. Many stone traps were set in order to catch otters until this was outlawed around 1980. Some of these large structures can still be seen standing around certain parts of the Shetland Islands even today, just above the high water level, though happily without a trap door attached.

Otters are usually freshwater creatures in mainland Britain, inhabiting our rivers and lakes, but in the Shetland Islands they have adapted to life in the harsher tidal environment and can be seen swimming and hunting happily in the islands' many seawater voes. The otters still require fresh water to wash the salt water out of their fur in order to keep it healthy, insulative and waterproof. In this regard otters can often be seen following the course of a small beck (called locally a 'burn') from the sea to some freshwater lake where they can wash, clean and play.

The Lord Jesus one day spoke to His disciples about cleanliness, saying, "Now ye are clean through the word which I have spoken unto you" (John ch15v3). Cleanliness is a very important part of the Christian life and must be taken seriously. The Lord Jesus was not talking about the outward washing of the body, such as having a bath or a shower, but the cleansing of our souls in order to make them fit for God's presence in Heaven. The Bible again speaks of *"the washing of water by the word"* (Ephesians ch5v26). What these verses are telling us is that the Bible, the Word of God, leads us to trusting the Lord Jesus as our Saviour and then daily keeps us clean and pure if we are prepared to read and practise what it says.

If you are fortunate to catch a glimpse of a family of otters, they are called collectively a *bevy*, a *family*, a *lodge* or, perhaps most descriptively of all, a *romp*, this last name obviously coming from the otter's playful habits both in and out of the water.

Otters measure around one to one and a half metres in length and can weigh anything between five and fifteen kilograms! Unlike the two seal species found in Shetland that look cumbersome and ungainly out of water, otters seem to be just as much at home on the shore as in the sea. They feed primarily on fish, however they will eat crab and other shellfish which they have become very adept at handling. Look for the occasional scarring of the nose and face of the otter where it has had a close encounter with a crab's claw whilst seeking its lunch!

Sailors, Storms and Shipwrecks

With so much water around the islands, and with a coastline of almost 1700 miles long, the history of wrecks in the seas around Shetland goes back almost as far as history itself! The first shipwrecks recorded were in the year 1148, when two Viking longships, the Hjolp and the Fifa, were wrecked, although the exact location is not fully known.

Perhaps one of the saddest accidents to occur around the islands was on Friday, 28th March 1930, when the thirty-one metre long fishing boat, Ben Doran, foundered on the Ve Skerries, just west of the island of Papa Stour. There were no radios for communication in those days, so the crew sent up rockets and waved distress flares in order to signal that they were in trouble. These were spotted on the Mainland but considered to be no more than a chimney on fire on Papa Stour!

Meanwhile, the trawler remained marooned on the rocks through the night until being spotted by another fishing boat, the Bracken Bush, at midday on Saturday. This trawler, unable to get close enough to help, made full speed to Hillswick in order to raise the alarm. Once the news was out that the boat was aground, many sought to help as best and as quickly as they could. There were nine fishermen on the stricken boat that needed to be rescued. The local coastguard made out with rescue apparatus in the hope of firing a line to the stricken vessel. Other brave men tried to row to the ship, but the worsening weather made getting any closer than several hundred metres almost impossible. Realising the severity of the situation, a call was made for the Orkney lifeboat to put out from Stromness, as there was at that time no lifeboat situated in any part of the Shetland Islands. The brave crew had been put on alert on Sunday morning but the order to set sail was sadly not given until Sunday night. They battled through the ever worsening seas between the Orkneys and Shetland all Sunday night, seeking to cover the one hundred and twenty miles that separates the two groups of islands as quickly as possible.

Meanwhile, on the scene of the wreck that was now being broken up at an ever alarming rate by the gale force winds and monstrous tides, were nine other boats, all eager to help save the crew of the Ben Doran. As they watched through the storm they could see that seven men had tied themselves to the rigging of the boat to keep from being washed off its continually swamped decks. Some witnesses said they could see the men moving and trying to keep warm as the wind, rain, waves and bitter cold tore at their bodies. Others believed that they had died there on the ship's mast, frozen to death by the constant soaking of sea and spray. The watching sailors saw with horror the mast bearing seven of the fishermen of the Ben Doran fall into the sea at around two o'clock on the afternoon of Sunday 30th and all watching knew that any hope of rescue was now gone.

Earlier a flying boat from Felixstowe in Suffolk had been scrambled with the intention of dropping rafts to the desperate crew. Flying north, the plane ran into bad weather and had to land in Invergordon, Inverness-shire to wait for the weather to clear. By the time it was able to take off again it was much too late.

Only three bodies were ever recovered, of which it was thought that two, being strong swimmers, had attempted to swim with a line from the Ben Doran to the closest of the rescue boats standing so near and yet so far away. One of these bodies, when discovered a week later, had a rope tied around his waist, the man's last thought and intention being to try and rescue his fellow sailors. These two brave men had battled waves of around fifteen metres in height, but sadly had not been strong enough to overcome the surging sea and as a result they had been lost. This amazing yet tragic story is still told with much emotion on the islands today and a monument to the men who perished was erected in the Sandness Cemetery on the west of the island.

Forty-seven years later on 9th December 1977, another trawler, the twenty-three metre long Elinor Viking, ran aground in exactly the same place in similar stormy conditions, but this time with a blinding blizzard to hinder all rescue attempts. The Aith lifeboat was called but due to the awful weather was unable to render the assistance the crew needed. A British Airways helicopter was scrambled from Sumburgh, manned by volunteers. Despite the storm force winds it arrived above the wreck and, due to the skill of the pilot and his crew, was able to winch everybody off the stricken boat to safety just fifteen minutes before the surging sea claimed another ship. The helicopter crew all received bravery awards for their gallant and heroic efforts.

These two stories with such different outcomes remind us so much of the message of the gospel as declared in the Bible. We are lost on the sea of sin with no hope of ever being able to get to Heaven as we are. Maybe all our friends think that they can help in some way, but all come short of the assistance we need to be rid of our sin and ready for Heaven. We may even try to 'swim' to safety by turning over a new leaf or trying to make ourselves better by changing our lives, however none of this is good enough to make us fit enough for God. Despite our dire and desperate need, God, in His great love, sent the Lord Jesus right to where we are. *"The Father sent the Son to be the Saviour of the world"* (1st John ch4v14). Just like the helicopter arriving in time over the Elinor Viking, so the Lord Jesus came to this earth in order to rescue us from above. If we are prepared to turn from our sin and trust Him as Saviour, He can and will save us from the storm of sin and make us fit for Heaven.

Oil Tankers and Oil Spills

Tuesday, 5th January 1993, is a day that will live in the memories of the Shetland Islanders for a long time. At twenty past five in the morning a distress call was sent out from the colossal oil tanker, Braer, with a crew of thirty-four and carrying 85,000 tonnes of oil, that the ship had lost power and was drifting in stormy seas ten miles south of Sumburgh Head at the southernmost tip of Shetland. This giant oil

Wreck of Oil Tanker MV Braer

tanker weighed 45,000 tonnes unladen, measured 242m long and was 40m wide! Three hours later the gale had increased to a force 10 or 11 and so the ship's captain and coastguard decided to commence helicopter evacuation of the ship's non-essential personnel, due to the fact that the ship was now being driven by the seas towards the southernmost coastline of Shetland. This was successfully carried out by the rescue helicopter flying out of Sumburgh, and fourteen of the crew were lifted safely off the giant ship.

In the meantime, tugs had been summoned to the area in the hope of fixing tow lines to the stricken tanker in order to pull it clear of the island's coast. The previous year a similar tanker, the Aegean Sea, had run aground and burst into flames in Galacia, Spain. Due to the ship's proximity to Horse Island to the west of Sumburgh Head, at eight fifty in the morning it was decided to abandon ship by rescuing all the crew by helicopter. This done, there was relief when the now crewless ship slipped past Horse Island without incident.

At around this time the oceangoing tug boat, Star Sirius, arrived on the scene and so the captain of the Braer and some of his crew were taken by helicopter to be put back onto the ship. They hoped that they would be able to establish a tow line from the tug which would then at least be able to pull the ship out of immediate danger. Sadly, despite everyone's best efforts, this failed and at eleven twenty the oil tanker Braer ran aground on the point of Garths Ness in the Bay of Quendale to the west of Sumburgh. The emergency crew were again rescued from the ship and, as oil could be observed spilling out of the huge tanks of the ship, containment and clean-up operations were immediately commenced to deal with what was obviously going to be a giant oil spill.

One of the biggest concerns for all involved was the great impact such an oil spill would have on the local wildlife population. The huge seabird colonies could be greatly affected due to the likelihood of birds becoming oiled by diving into the oil covered seas in search of fish. They would then be unable to fly and therefore unable to help themselves. The internationally important otter population was also at great risk from such an environmental catastrophe. Various organisations set up rescue centres where ill and oiled birds and mammals could be taken in order to be treated, cleaned and cared for before release back into the wild.

Meanwhile, back at Garths Ness, the wreck of the great ship was taking a huge pounding from the gale force winds that were whipping up giant waves that crashed over the once proud tanker. Eventually the onlookers watching from the cliffs above the wreck saw the ship break in two as the wind and waves exacted a huge toll on the manmade monster of the seas. Within a month all that was left to be seen was the massive bow section sticking out of the sea like a huge metal rock pointing up to the heavens. Within a year the frequent storms and high tides of Shetland had claimed all of the once mighty Braer and it had slid silently below the mighty ocean as another sad statistic of wrecks around these treacherous shores.

Thankfully for all concerned, the oil being carried on the Braer was of a lighter type than was usually found on such ships and with the repeated gales and high seas that lashed the coast throughout January 1993 it was soon broken up by the natural force of the wind, weather, waves and water, so the huge environmental disaster that it could have been was averted. Local people, even those living twenty or more miles away, still talk of having to wipe oil off their house windows after it had been carried inland by the gale force winds.

Although the impact environmentally was not as bad as expected, the statistics of wildlife casualties as a result of the disaster make for sad and distressing reading. In the weeks following the wreck, over 1500 dead seabirds were recovered from the beaches and coastline around southern Shetland. This, of course, does not account for the bodies of seabirds and mammals that were never washed ashore but were taken out by the tide to be lost forever at sea.

The wreck and resulting environmental damage of the Braer accident should remind us of the impact of our own sin and rebellion against God, not only upon ourselves, but on others as well. So often our sin of selfishness, cheek, wanting our own way, name-calling or tale-telling can affect others in as big a way as ourselves. The pollution of our sin grows and if not dealt with will pollute and contaminate those around us as well as ourselves. Thankfully we know that there is an answer to this great problem we all have. There is a cleansing agent that can permanently remove every part of our sin's pollution. The Bible states that *"the blood of Jesus Christ His (God's) Son cleanseth us from all sin"* (1st John ch1v7). Yes, the precious blood of the Lord Jesus, that flowed when He died on the cross, is enough to remove every sin we have ever or will ever commit if we are prepared to trust Him as Saviour and allow Him to take control of our lives.

Another Titanic Disaster

RMS (Royal Mail Ship) Oceanic was launched on 14th January 1899 and had her maiden voyage on 6th September the same year. At the time of her building Oceanic was the largest passenger ship in the world. Weighing in at a very impressive 17,272 tonnes and costing in excess of one million pounds she rightly claimed the title "Queen of the Ocean". This two funnelled giant of the seas was built by the White Star Line, the company that twelve years after her launch would own and sail perhaps the most famous ship of all time - the Titanic. Oceanic, like Titanic later, was fitted out with every conceivable luxury available and was capable of carrying over 2000

RMS Oceanic

passengers with 400 travelling first class in grand style, 300 second class and over 1000 third class. She was 700 feet long and 68 feet wide; by today's standards not huge, but at the time of building she was a giant of the seas.

In 1901 Oceanic had a collision with a much smaller vessel, the SS Kincora, in very thick fog. This was an accident that resulted in the Kincora sinking with the loss of seven of her crew.

In 1912 the Oceanic was at sea when she received the distress call from the Titanic. Although not close enough to render any immediate assistance, she did arrive on the scene the next day and commenced a search of the area, picking up several bodies and other items from the sunken vessel.

After nearly fifteen years of service plying the seas mostly between Britain and America, she was commissioned for wartime use at the outbreak of the First World War in 1914. On 8th August 1914 the Oceanic, now known as HMS Oceanic, and having been fitted out as an armed merchant cruiser, began work for the Royal Navy. On 25th August the ship set sail for Lerwick having several hundred Royal Marines aboard with the intention of patrolling the waters around the Shetland Islands and as far west as the Faroes in order to intercept any German registered boats that may have been sailing in the area.

Little did anyone realize at the time but the mighty Oceanic's Royal Navy career would last just two weeks.

As she sailed for Shetland she had two captains on board - one from the Navy and the other her original captain from her time as a passenger ship. She sailed northwards continually zigzagging across the sea in an attempt to avoid any German U-boats that may have been looking for a fairly large and easy target. On 7th September Oceanic left Lerwick and headed round the islands and out towards Faroe. The two captains at this point appear to have had a disagreement about which side of the island of Foula to sail, her civilian captain opting to steer to the west and into the open sea, but the Navy captain overruling the good judgement of his more experienced counterpart and seeking to sail between Foula and the Shetland mainland. This was a fatal mistake as Oceanic ran straight into the Shaalds reef just east of Foula. It was a tragic decision, resulting in the once mighty Oceanic coming to grief on rocks in good weather and on a calm sea.

A trawler from Aberdeen, the Glenogil, was the first on the scene, and, having initially tried in vain to tow the massive liner off the rocks, opted to take everyone off the stricken vessel to safety. The last of the four hundred people to be rescued was the first officer, one Charles Lightoller, who had been the most senior officer to survive the sinking of the Titanic. This was not to be his last wreck as he would experience two more before the end of the First World War!

All were brought safely to shore and, two weeks later, on the night of 29th September during a howling gale, the once majestic Oceanic slipped unobserved off the Shaalds reef and to the bottom of the ocean.

How much the loss of this great ship can teach us! The two captains disagreeing over which way the ship should go and such confusion ending in total disaster. How good it is to remember the words of the Lord Jesus, *"One is your Master, even Christ"* (Matthew ch23v8). If we allow the Lord Jesus to be our Lord and Master we know that we will never founder on the awful reefs of sin. We know too that He knows the right way to God far better than we do, for He said, *"I am the Way, the Truth, and the Life: no man cometh unto the Father, but by Me"* (John ch14v6). He is not only the guide into Heaven, but the only way to Heaven for those who will trust Him as Lord and Saviour.

Longboats and Longhouses

Viking Longboat

Although only small in comparison to Scandinavian countries like Denmark and Norway, for the Viking warriors heading west from their own countries in search of new places to capture and conquer,

Shetland was the nearest land. On approaching Shetland with its various voes and sounds, the Viking raiders could have been forgiven for thinking that the islands looked very much like their own homelands with their mighty fjords and valleys. It is believed that the Vikings arrived in Shetland around 800AD in their fantastic and futuristic longships, made by riveting long wooden planks together. These ships were extremely well built, having a keel to help keep them stable and this, along with an efficient crew, helped them to cope well with the often vicious and dangerous sea currents around the islands. These incredible boats varied in size, between fifteen and thirty metres in length, although always narrow at about two and a half to three metres wide. The boats had benches for the oarsmen to sit upon and could hold around forty to eighty people; however some of the boats were fitted with boxes instead of benches, which were able to provide more storage space for any cargo being carried. Their unique design, having a bow section at both ends, meant that they could quickly change direction if required by going in reverse with no loss of speed. They also had a very shallow draft (depth when in the water) allowing them to manoeuvre up very shallow stretches of water, perhaps only one metre deep! These boats were also very light for their size, allowing a crew to carry them easily onto shore when required. Under full power they could travel at between five and fifteen knots which is incredibly fast for a boat without a motor! Later they introduced sails so that on long journeys the rowers were able to relax and have a break as the wind bore the craft and its occupants along. It has been estimated that these sails could be up to twelve metres wide; they were made of woven wool, and could be raised or lowered up the ship's mast as and when required. The Vikings were also able to navigate exceptionally well by using the sun and stars as guides.

Once on the islands these Norsemen commenced working the land and building homes suitable to withstand the harsh Shetland winters. These houses are called 'longhouses' and the remains of many of them can be seen scattered throughout the length of the islands even today. The simple but strong homes could be up to seventy-five metres in length and seven metres wide, with just a single room, providing plenty of space for working, sleeping, cooking or relaxing. Many were built low to the ground so as to provide the least wind resistance to the fierce gales that are known to howl around the islands in the dark winter months. These houses were built of stone and the cavities filled with mud and peat. The roof was made of either a type of thatch or with cut turfs of grass. In this roof was a hole that allowed smoke from the fire used for heating and cooking to escape. Due to the roof's construction it would have to be changed or repaired occasionally, just as thatched houses have to be even today. Once built, many were lined with wood to make them more homely and warm. As any visitor to the islands will notice there is a great lack of trees and it is thought that the Norsemen sent back home to Norway in order to obtain the wood needed for their new homes. Around the sides of the room were benches, often covered with animal skins in order to give a little more comfort, and most of the occupants slept on these, using them as beds as well as seats. There were no windows in these longhouses so the only light came from the door, the hole in the roof or during the night from the fire.

It is thought that the better-off families would have divided their homes into different rooms using curtains, whereas poorer families would also have had to share their accommodation with their animals. This would at least have helped to keep the room warmer in winter, if not a little smellier!

The Lord Jesus one day spoke of two builders who each wanted to build a house. One looked carefully for a good foundation on a solid rock, whereas the other, more careless, builder just sought the best position, possibly with good views, upon the sand. Once they had finished building and their homes were completed both moved into their new houses, no doubt pleased with all their hard work. However, not too long afterwards a great storm blew up, and whilst the house built upon the rock stood firm and strong, the one built upon the sand fell, unable to withstand the wind, rain and waves. The Lord Jesus told this story as a warning to us to think seriously about where we are building our lives, for He said, *"Whosoever heareth these sayings of mine, and doeth them, I will liken him unto a wise man, which built his house upon a rock: and the rain descended, and the floods came, and the winds blew, and beat upon that house; and it fell not: for it was founded upon a rock"* (Matthew ch7v24+25). Are we living on the uncertain foundation of this world and what it has to offer or the certain hope of Heaven, by building our lives around the wonderful Person of the Lord Jesus?

The Strongest Horse in the World

Travel around the islands and you will see in the fields, at almost every turn, the wonderful little horse that just about everyone loves – the Shetland pony! These small, short-legged, thick-coated, incredibly strong and highly intelligent animals originate from these islands, and are ideal for braving some of the worst weather found anywhere in the British Isles. They stand at 70 to 120cm in height to their shoulders (seven to eleven hands in horse language) and can be used for riding, carrying or just as a helpful and friendly pet.

In Shetland these ponies were ideal for pulling carts and hauling peat dug for fuel for fires and stoves in crofting communities. During the Victorian age, when coal mining boomed in the United Kingdom, many of these ponies were taken south to work deep underground due to their great strength and small size. Here they were kept in very poor conditions for most of their lives which, sadly, were often very short. People living close to these coal mines tell of seeing the ponies frisking about in the fields on the rare occasions they were

Shetland Pony

allowed out of their darkened underground prison to exercise in the open paddocks close to the mines. Thankfully these beautiful ponies are no longer cruelly used in such a way.

Shetland ponies certainly have personality and make great first ponies or pets for children. They are noted as being brave little animals, not shying away from frightening situations. They are good natured and have a good temperament towards people. Just stop next to any field containing these wonderful creatures and you will see how they will

49

wander over to you for a pat, stroke and fuss and also, no doubt, in the hope of receiving some nice titbit treat from kind and generous humans! Like most animals, Shetland ponies do need to be well trained or they can become very cheeky! Shetland ponies are noted for occasionally having a 'stubborn streak', but this can usually be blamed on poor ownership rather than on the animal's temperament.

There lived in the days of Moses a very unusual man by the name of Balaam, whose life was saved by the stubbornness of his donkey! Balaam claimed to be a prophet of the Lord but the New Testament makes it clear that Balaam was really a false prophet and not a true prophet of God at all. One of the kings living at that time was afraid of Moses and the nation of Israel as they passed through his land, so he asked Balaam to curse the Israelites who were under Moses' command, promising Balaam great wealth if he did this. To his credit, Balaam did ask God what to do, but when God told him he must not curse the Israelites as they were God's chosen people, Balaam stupidly decided to disobey God and carry on regardless, seeking the money of Balak the king rather than the message of God. He started to ride on his donkey to meet Balak but God put His angel in the way to stop Balaam from doing what was so clearly wrong. Balaam could not see the angel, but his donkey saw it, and, having run into a field, trapped Balaam's foot against a wall in an attempt to flee the angel. Eventually the donkey sat down and refused to move. Balaam was so mad with the stubbornness of his donkey that he hit it each time it tried to get out of the angel's way. Then as the donkey sat on the ground an astonishing thing happened! The donkey started to speak and asked Balaam why he had hit her on three occasions. Amazingly, Balaam spoke back to the donkey, saying, *"I would there were a sword in mine hand, for now would I kill thee"* (Numbers ch22v29). It was then that the Lord opened Balaam's eyes so that he too could see the angel. He realised then that despite his cruelty to his donkey it had actually saved his life.

Poor Balaam! Despite God's warnings to him he still continued on the wrong road until, as Peter puts it in the New Testament, *"The dumb [donkey] speaking with man's voice forbad (stopped) the madness of the prophet"* (2nd Peter ch2v16). How often do we, like Balaam, keep on the wrong road despite all God's efforts to get us to turn around and start going the right way? King Solomon wrote one day that *"There is a way that seemeth right unto a man, but the end thereof are the ways of death"* (Proverbs ch16v25). The Lord Jesus said, *"I am the way"* (John ch14v6), very clearly showing that He is the only way to Heaven for those who trust Him as Saviour.

It seems to be a little known fact that Shetland ponies, for their size, are actually the strongest of all horse breeds! A Shetland pony is more than able to pull twice its own weight, whereas the huge shire horses that you may sometimes see are only able to pull half their own body weight. Shetland ponies can also carry riders up to 60kg, which is no mean feat for an animal of such small stature. I suppose that these amazing statistics make the little often-overlooked Shetland pony something of a superhorse in the equine world!

As you travel round the islands look out for the beautiful little horses and see how many different coloured ones you can spot. You will soon notice that they come in a huge range of colours, although you are unlikely to see them in blue or red unless it's either an exceptionally cold or hot day!

Woolly Sheep and Woolly Jumpers

You can hardly miss them, for Shetland sheep are everywhere - in fields, on the cliff tops, across the heather and even wandering over the roads... well, do try to miss these! Actually, it does seem that most sheep in Shetland do have very good road sense. But don't take it for granted, especially on the single track roads when one might unexpectedly decide to make a dash ahead of your car.

It is estimated that there are about 350,000 sheep that live there. That equates to fifteen sheep to every person living in Shetland. Folks living here obviously don't have too much trouble sleeping with all those sheep to count at night!

The first thing that you will notice about these sheep is that they are generally much smaller than the usual British breeds, weighing only about 20 to 25kg, although Shetland sheep bred in the warmer climes of Britain may be much larger. They are an incredibly hardy breed and, believe it or not, can stay out on the hills and moors all year round in all weathers. They can also survive very well eating the poorer vegetation that is found on the higher heather slopes of the islands, especially in winter, although most of the croft farmers who tend them will add supplementary feed to their diet. Their lambs are born much later than in mainland Britain, usually at the end of April or the beginning of May when the cold winter weather has truly gone. The breed is so hardy that the lambs are usually born out in the fields or in the hills and require little or no human help. The lambs are able to get up almost right away and feed and, unlike some of the less hardy varieties, have a good inbred will to live which gives them great survival attributes. Because the sheep are smaller they are generally easier to handle and make for great breeds on a smaller farm or croft. Take a quick look behind the sheep and you may notice

Shetland Sheep

Woolly Sheep and Woolly Jumpers

(if you're an expert in sheep watching) that the tails of these sheep are much shorter than other breeds. Without doubt the Shetland sheep is a unique animal in the sheep stakes!

When watching the shepherd going out into the hills in order to provide the sheep the extra feed that they need, you will often see the sheep flock round the shepherd, knowing that he is showing his care for them by bringing good food to them. The Lord Jesus used the example of being a shepherd when He said, *"I am the Good Shepherd: the Good Shepherd giveth His life for the sheep"* (John ch10v11). The Lord Jesus wants the very best for us and so He gave His life upon the cross so that we (the sheep) could have our sins forgiven and cleansed, making us fit for heaven. He went on to say, *"My sheep hear My voice, and I know them, and they follow Me"* (John ch10v27). Have you heard the Lord's voice calling and asking you to follow Him and be saved?

In many fields across Shetland, especially in the higher, more exposed areas, you will often see large circular stone structures with an opening somewhere around its circumference. These are sheep shelters provided by the crofters to provide protection for the sheep. Amazingly, the sheep are sensible enough to enter these in order to find shelter and warmth together when the weather turns stormy or when there is a blizzard blowing.

55

The fleece (woolly coat) of this breed is usually lost in spring and often the wool can be plucked off by hand (called rooed) without the use of shears. This is said to make the wool softer as it is all natural with no cut threads such as those which occur with sheared sheep. The wool from these sheep is declared to be the finest in the world. As somebody once said, Shetland wool has "the gloss and softness of silk, the strength of cotton, the whiteness of linen and the warmth of wool."

This wool comes in many natural colours of which there are apparently eleven with a further thirty different types of markings recognised officially. With all these colours and variations of wool available it allows the skilled knitter to produce a range of totally natural knitwear; the 'Fair Isle' produce from Shetland is world famous.

Hunters of the Deep

Have you ever come face to face with a real sea monster? How about getting close to a merciless killer? Well, if that sort of adventure appeals to you, welcome to Shetland, the home of murderously powerful sea monsters known as orcas or, to most of us, killer whales. It is interesting when studying these giant but fascinating creatures to realise that

Orca

they are actually the largest members of the oceanic dolphin family, which contains thirty-five species! This grouping means that the orca is more closely related to the dolphin than to other whales. How about that - killer dolphins, whatever next? The killer whale has no predators and rarely attacks humans in the wild unless you get a bit too close for its liking. So keep on shore or in a boat and at the right time you may just catch a sight of one of these awesome and powerful creatures.

Orcas have black backs and white fronts that extend round the sides giving a very distinct black and white appearance. They also have a white patch just behind the eye. They all have a dorsal fin, which is most possibly what you will see first in any sightings you have. This can be up to two metres tall and is triangular in shape on the bull (male) and curved in the cow (female). They can grow to seven or eight metres in length for a bull and weigh over eight tonnes, whereas the cow is slightly shorter at five to seven metres and weighs only three or four tonnes. The orca is one of the fastest marine mammals in the world and can get up to a speed of 30 knots - that's a very impressive 56km/h! Don't try out-swimming one, will you?

It would seem that, as with seals, the females outlive the males by some considerable time as they average around fifty years compared to the males' thirty years, although much older cases have been reported. The calves (babies) can be born at any time of the year but research has shown that mothers only have one calf about every five years. This calf is looked after by the whole pod (group) of whales for its first two years until it is properly able to look after and care for itself. It would seem that female killer whales breed between the ages of fifteen and forty years of age.

Although they have been observed in deeper seas, orcas seem to prefer shallower depths, often coming close to the shore in order to catch their prey. It has been estimated that killer whales require about 230kg of food every day - that's a lot of food and a lot of calories! Orcas mainly eat fish, often working as a group in order to catch large quantities. This behaviour gives rise to the name 'wolves of the sea' due to their wolf pack instincts. Surprisingly, other whales are also eaten, and even much bigger ones may be attacked and killed by a pod who often drown their chosen prey by not allowing them to the surface of the water to breath. In Shetland they regularly target seals who are unfortunate enough to come into the path of these great killers of the deep. It has also been observed (though not in Shetland) that occasionally they will throw themselves out of the water and onto the land (called 'beaching') in order to pull some poor unsuspecting seal off its resting place and then with a wriggling motion return back into the sea with its spoil.

Yes, there is no doubt about it, whales are large and fascinating creatures but with a built-in killer instinct that will stop at nothing to get its prey. The Bible warns of a great enemy that we all need to be aware of and deal with if we are going to live lives pleasing to the Lord Jesus and go to Heaven. This enemy is called sin and it is very dangerous if we are not on the alert for, or aware of, its great danger. The Bible states that *"sin, when it is finished, bringeth forth death"* (James ch1v15) and *"the wages of sin is death"* (Romans ch6v23). However, we can be sure that if we have the Lord Jesus Christ as our Saviour He will watch over us and keep us from the danger and damage this cruel enemy can do, for the Bible says that Christians are *"kept by the power of God"* (1st Peter ch1v5).

Flags and Allegiances

The Shetland flag is perhaps one of the newest in the world, only being officially recognised in 2005. The story, however, goes back to the year 1969, which marked the five hundredth anniversary of the pawning of Shetland from Norway to Scotland. This came about in a most unusual way. In 1469, the King of Denmark and Norway's daughter wanted to marry the King of Scotland's son. It was the custom at that time

Shetland Flag

for the daughter's father to pay what was known as a dowry (a sort of marriage fee) to the father of his future son-in-law. The King of Denmark and Norway was not well off so he offered both the Shetland and the Orkney Islands to the King of Scotland with a provision that any future richer king could buy the islands back again. This sadly led to the rich Scottish landowners using their great wealth and power to steal the land from the native Shetlanders and then extorting large taxes from anyone who was using the land they had taken. The Scottish lairds and officials became more cruel and oppressive towards the native islanders as they grabbed more and more land for themselves. The Shetlanders were controlled by these cruel taskmasters until a Crofting Act finally became law, giving the crofters of Shetland the rights and protection they needed from these bullying landlords.

In order to mark the five hundredth anniversary of this event some of the islanders were keen to see a Shetland flag designed that could be proudly flown over the islands. Two young students, studying in Aberdeen, decided to design a flag that represented both the islands' past and present. They looked at the Danish flag of a white cross on a red background and the Scottish saltire of a diagonal white cross on a blue background. They took the two flags and made a new one with a blue background to symbolise Scotland and a straight white cross to symbolise their Scandinavian past. It was an incredibly simple idea, yet very clever. The flag was not, however, fully accepted right away as various other ideas were suggested. In the course of time the idea gained popularity and the Shetland flag was used for the first time to represent the islands in the Island games (a type of Olympic games for small islands) held in the Isle of Man during 1985. From then on the flag was used to promote Shetland products and tourism, was seen on Shetland based boats and flown from some islanders' homes. It was time for the authorities to act and officially recognise this new island emblem. There were laws made and passed to adopt this flag as the islands' national emblem and this came into being in 2005. In 2007, on 21st June, the longest day of the year when the sun hardly sets at all on Shetland, the islanders proclaimed it 'Shetland Flag day' which was the commencement of an annual event on that date every year.

It must have been quite an unforgettable experience for the inhabitants of the Shetland Islands in 1469 to be told that they were changing nationality from belonging to the Scandinavian countries to that of Scotland. How sad it must have been, though, to discover that they could be treated in such a cruel and tyrannical way by their new owners! Many never forgot what happened at that time and much is still remembered even today. Thankfully this is nothing like salvation for the Christian who has repented of their sins and trusted the Lord Jesus as their Saviour. They never forget the time and place where that change took place because it was so wonderful and good. The great apostle Paul gave his story of conversion at least twice throughout the book of the Acts in the Bible as it was so important and real to him. In writing to Timothy and telling about this great event he said twice that there had been a day when he *"obtained mercy"* (1st Timothy ch1v13+16), before continuing to explain about the great work of the Lord Jesus. *"This is a faithful saying, and worthy of all acceptation, that Christ Jesus came into the world to save sinners"* (1st Timothy ch1v15). The day Paul was saved was a day that he never forgot. He wanted to tell everyone about as it was so real to him. It was as if he had a new flag flying over his life saying to all around, 'I used to be a sinner but now I belong to the Lord Jesus!'

Seabirds and Seashores

You cannot visit these wonderful islands without noticing that there are many seabirds. In fact, the islands are full of them. It has been estimated that around one million seabirds use these islands for either nesting and rearing young or as a passage route as they migrate around the world. There is no doubt about it; the Shetland Islands are a place like no other if you have the slightest interest in ornithology (bird watching) at all. The great thrill of being able to stand on the top of one of the islands' sheer cliffs and be overawed by the noise and constant motion of these massive seabird colonies is hard to beat. Here you will see many different species of birds, all in their natural environment, where normally you would need to travel perhaps hundreds of miles in order to observe them all on the British mainland. It's a wonderful paradise of winged wonders and feathered frenzy unrivalled throughout most of the world.

Ornithologists are divided as to which are the best seabird sites. Perhaps most would choose the cliffs of Noss, just off the island of Bressay which lies opposite the capital, Lerwick. Two short ferry crossings will bring you to this now uninhabited island where a walk along the cliff paths will furnish you with a sight that will long live on in your memory. Walk to Noup of Noss, the most easterly part, to view the spectacular two hundred metre high cliffs as they plunge almost vertically down to the sea. See how even in the midst of the endless activity of the avian wonders there appears to be an order and structure about their high rise existence. On the cliff's top are the burrows used by the puffins to nest and raise their young.

Now look further down to see the large and beautiful gannet colonies set up in their somewhat precarious-looking nesting sites, high up on

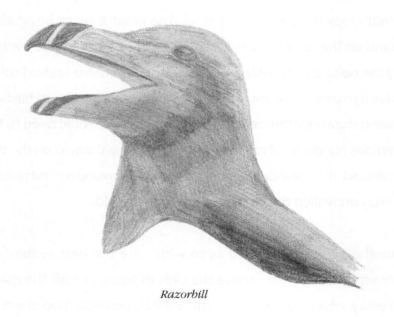

Razorbill

the ledges in the cliffs. These impressive black and white birds with their distinctive yellow head are the largest seabirds in the northern hemisphere, with a wingspan of up to two metres. The gannet can dive into the water from a height of thirty metres, often hitting the sea at a speed of 100km/h! They fold in their wings completely just prior to impact with the water, making their bodies extremely streamlined, enabling them to swim to great depths in search of their favourite food – fish. It is estimated that there are about 30,000 gannets living on Shetland, which is about two thirds of the world's population.

Nesting on the cliffs below the gannets you will see the guillemots and razorbills which are both, like the puffin, members of the auk family. Again you may find up to 140,000 guillemots around these coasts, however don't try to count them all, will you? The guillemot is very similar in looks to the razorbill but has a browner back and a sharper, much more pointed, beak that gives its head and whole body a sleeker look than that of the razorbill. Guillemots spend most of their time at sea and only come ashore in order to breed.

The razorbill, with its distinctive black back, white belly and large, blunt, black beak with a single white flash giving it its name, is slightly larger than the puffin. Razorbills are unusual in that they will catch and eat their food whilst underwater. They do not build a nest but just lay a single egg on the rock. The parent birds then take turns in incubating the egg. They will fly many kilometres away from the nest site in search of suitable food and, like the puffin, have the ability to hold several fish in their beaks all at the same time.

Lastly, down at the very bottom of the cliffs, just about the level of the sea, you will find some big black birds called shags. These birds are members of the cormorant family and can be seen in coastal areas across much of the British Mainland. You may find cormorants in inland lakes elsewhere but shags will always be found around salt water. The main way to distinguish the two is to look for the white patch around the beak of the cormorant which the shag does not have. It is not always easy, however, to spot this distinguishing feature. One thing that both these birds do is sit with their wings held out either side of their bodies as if trying to dry them. Unlike the gannet, shags dive into the water from a swimming, not a flying, position, often commencing a dive with a little jump, but despite this they have been recorded at depths of 45m in their search for food.

Look up into the skies and you may be fortunate enough to spot the distinctive, but totally amazing, Arctic tern as it zips through the air, occasionally diving into the sea after some small fish. These medium sized birds fly from the Arctic to the Antarctic and back every year, covering a distance of around 71,000km! No other bird or mammal covers such a great distance. They land only occasionally to breed and this may be once every one to three years as they eat, sleep and feed whilst continually flying around the world. They are marked by another feature too – longevity. They have been known to live up to thirty years, which is a long time for a bird. They obviously keep fit with all that travelling! When observing this magnificent bird you can only be awestruck that such a small creature could be designed for such a life of globetrotting.

Lastly, if you're prepared to head north and catch the ferry from Yell to the island of Fetlar, you may well come across the oddly named red-necked phalarope. This beautiful orange-red necked little bird only measures about 18cm in length but is another winged wonder. These birds are different to most other bird types in that the female lays the eggs and immediately flies off south, leaving the male bird to incubate and bring up the young alone. To watch them swimming around flitting here and there brings a smile to the face as they move busily in search of any little insects that may be on offer. They also swim round in complete circles very quickly in shallow water, making a vortex that brings food from the water's bottom to the surface, which they then swiftly pick up with their delicate, but long, pointed beaks. These, like many other seabirds, only come ashore in order to breed, spending the rest of their time at sea.

The Lord Jesus once told His disciples to *"Behold the fowls of the air:*

for they sow not, neither do they reap, nor gather into barns; yet your heavenly Father feedeth them. Are ye not much better than they?" (Matthew ch6v26). The Lord was showing God's care for all these wonderful birds that we have considered. As He is the Creator of them all, He knows each one and cares for them by providing food suitable for each type. In another place the Lord said that God knows when one sparrow falls to the ground and dies. How much greater then is His love towards us in sending His Son to die on a cross to save us. *"But God commendeth His love toward us, in that, while we were yet sinners, Christ died for us"* (Romans ch5v8).

Pirates of the Air

The only way you will miss this large bird is if you walk around with your eyes shut! At over half a metre in length and with a wingspan of nearly one and a half metres, it looks like a very large brown seagull. Its wings, however, are much more rounded than those of seagulls and have white flashes on the undersides. Although its feet are webbed they have claws similar to a bird of prey. It has a large grey beak with a big sharp hook at the end and a mean-looking face. This is the great skua, or the bronxie, as it is known locally.

Great Skua

The skua is a real pirate of the air, as it gains much of its food by attacking and robbing other birds of their catches. A favourite trick of this tyrant of the sky is to fly underneath a gannet and catch one of its wings in its beak. This causes the gannet to stall and fall to the ground or into the water where the skua attacks it until it gives up its prey. The only birds which great skuas fear are the golden eagle and the white-tailed sea eagle, although there have been records of several skuas attacking these bigger birds in a group. They will even attack and kill other seabirds, including those as big as a black-backed gull, which are very sizeable. Often they will swoop down on the nesting sites of terns and other easily accessible breeding places in order to steal the baby chicks from the nests of these birds. The terns will use their best efforts to drive the skua away, usually by collectively dive-bombing the skua and hitting it with their feet as well as pecking ferociously at it with their beaks. Sadly, due to its huge size and brute strength, these attempts are usually futile and the skua flies away carrying a little chick in its beak. Skuas have also been known to attack and kill adult puffins by diving upon them as they swim in the sea and drowning them by holding them underwater. They have also been observed waiting on cliff tops for birds to emerge from their nest sites before dropping down upon their unsuspecting victim. However, they do occasionally fish for themselves, enjoying sandeels which they catch near the shore where they swim close to the surface.

Great skuas have been known to attack people, diving aggressively at them with great force should they stray too close to their nesting sites which are just scrapings made in the moorland in which they lay their eggs. They can give a nasty whack with their wings if you are unfortunate enough to come into direct contact with them. They have also been known to chase off dogs that have come too close for comfort. So these birds are definitely best viewed from a distance.

In the Bible we read of an angel called Lucifer who one day rebelled against God and had to be thrown out of Heaven. Lucifer has ever since been known as the devil or Satan. Like the skua he will seek to attack whom he can so as to ruin their lives and prevent them from being in Heaven for eternity. He is called *"the prince of the power of the air"* (Ephesians ch2v2). The Bible warns us to *"be sober, be vigilant; because your adversary the devil, as a roaring lion, walketh about, seeking whom he may devour"* (1st Peter ch5 v8). If we are Christians we need to be careful of his attacks which can sometimes come without warning and cause us great spiritual harm. The Bible instructs us to *"submit yourselves therefore to God. Resist the devil, and he will flee from you"* (James ch4v7).

The Shetland Bus!

I'm sorry to say, but if you want to catch the Shetland Bus you are many years too late! Actually, this was not a conventional bus at all, such as we are used to seeing on our roads, but the name of a very important supply line between these islands and Norway during the war.

In the early hours of 9th April 1940, German forces commenced an invasion of Norway and Denmark, codenamed Operation Weserubung. With both these countries now occupied, Germany had wonderful new harbours and deep water fjords in which to anchor many of its great battleships. It also had the advantage of having possession of Norway's hundreds of miles of coastline from which to control its U-boat (submarine) fleet.

The British Special Operations Executive (SOE) was keen to land secret agents in Norway with a view to finding out what the situation was like there and what the German army was doing. It also wanted to help supply materials and ammunition to those in Norway who opposed the German occupation of their country. These people were known as resistance or underground workers or in Norway simply as 'The Ling'. Most of the British agents sent to Norway worked closely with these people. In 1941 a supply chain was set up using Norwegian fishing boats that had come to Shetland to escape the German invasion. These boats were mostly manned by Norwegian fishermen and were used for crossing to Norway in order to drop off agents and vital supplies without attracting German attention. For this, the boat crews were paid £4 per week with a £10 bonus for each successful trip they undertook.

Eventually, due to great loss of both boats and men, in October 1943 America provided three super-fast submarine chasing boats, thirty metres long and capable of twice the speed of the original fishing boats. At this point the whole operation working between the islands and Norway became part of the Norwegian Royal Navy.

During the time of the war the Shetland Bus made nearly 200 trips to occupied Norway, carrying nearly 200 agents and 400 tonnes of weapons for the Norwegian resistance fighters. They also returned 73 agents as well as rescuing 373 refugees whose lives were in danger if they remained in Norway. In carrying out all these trips forty-four men from the group died in action. These operations took place mostly in the winter time when the nights were longest and the seas roughest in order to escape German detection.

Tirpitz

One of the most daring actions which the Shetland Bus undertook was an attempt to sink the giant German battleship, the Tirpitz, which was anchored in Asenfjord in Norway some sixty miles inland from the coast. A plan was hatched to use human torpedoes (like a submarine upon which a man in wetsuit and breathing equipment rode) called chariots, to travel underwater to the great ship. They would then lay mines under its keel which, when they exploded, would sink the ship. A boat called the Arthur was loaded with peat, which was commonly transported by ship around Norway, the crew were given false papers and they set off on 26th October 1943. The boat was equipped to carry the torpedoes and had special areas built around the engine into which those who would ride the chariots to their target could hide if the Germans stopped and searched the boat. The chariots were initially strapped to the deck of the Arthur for the crossing from Shetland to Norway before being lowered into the water and slung underneath the boat to avoid detection by the German authorities.

After a slow two day crossing in very rough seas, the Arthur's engine broke down at the Norwegian coast. The crew skilfully handled the craft despite its engine troubles and moved closer to their intended target, having spent nearly a day securing the chariots in position under the boat. Further up the fjord the engine once again gave them problems, necessitating the crew calling at the village of Hestvik where they knew of a secret agent who could help them. This he did and repairs were made that enabled the Arthur to continue its journey up towards the Tirpitz.

Early on the morning of 31st October, the Arthur left Hestvik on the last part of its journey. Two hours later a German patrol boat stopped them, and having checked their papers and made a quick visual inspection, let them continue on their way. When the boat neared the Tirpitz the weather worsened and as the men who would ride the chariots to the target were getting into their frogman suits they could hear the chariots being bumped against the side of the boat by the now roughening water. It was not too long after that a huge noise was heard and the boat shuddered as something hit one of the engines. All knew that one of the torpedoes must have broken loose in the storm and hit the boat's propeller. The men stopped the Arthur whilst one of the frogmen dived below to check the damage and the state of the other chariot. All were sorely disappointed when he resurfaced to report that neither chariot was there anymore as both had broken off in the storm. They were only ten miles from the Tirpitz but now had no means of getting to it in order to place the charges that would have sunk her.

The Arthur would never be able to get them home so it was sunk and the ten man crew set off on foot in two groups for Sweden. Nine of the ten made it safely back but one man was shot by two German policemen who questioned the group. After a brief shootout the two policemen were killed and the four men, believing their colleague to be dead, left him and continued to Sweden. But Bob Evans was not dead. The Germans found him and rushing him to hospital managed to safe his life. Once well enough he was interrogated by the German authorities and on the command of General Keitel, the senior German general, was shot as a spy. It was this command that helped to convict General Keitel of crimes against humanity after the war and led to him being hanged. All nine remaining saboteurs arrived safely in Sweden, which was not involved in the war, and were eventually sent back to Scotland.

An interesting monument to the Shetland Bus, adorned by a fishing boat, can be seen overlooking Pund Voe on Main Street in Shetland's second largest community, Scalloway.

We can only guess at the disappointment of the men involved in the Shetland Bus operation in losing their chariots and being unable to complete their mission to sink the Tirpitz. How sad they must have felt at being so near but so far from success. The Bible warns that greater disappointment will come to those who leave God's salvation too late for *"now is the accepted time; behold, now is the day of salvation"* (2nd Corinthians ch6v2). If we are not ready in time there will be a day of huge sadness, deep regret and bitter disappointment that we have missed out on the opportunity of getting right with God and therefore spending forever in Heaven, for in that day, the Lord Jesus said, *"There shall be weeping and gnashing of teeth, when ye shall see Abraham, and Isaac, and Jacob, and all the prophets, in the kingdom of God, and you yourselves thrust out"* (Luke ch13v28).

Up Helly Aa

Do you enjoy a good bonfire on Bonfire Night on the 5th November? So did the Vikings, only they held theirs on the 24th night after Christmas and called it Yule. It was to celebrate the rebirth of the sun and the end of winter.

This festival is now held on the last Tuesday in January and is called Up Helly Aa or the 'Fire Festival' and it lasts all day. In the morning a huge proclamation called 'The Bill' is placed at Market Cross in the centre of Lerwick. This contains poems, news and other pieces of trivial information. Then, at ten o'clock in the morning, a 10 metre long longboat (called a Galley), which has been built by one of the islands' communities, is carried through the town to the sea front where it sits on display all day. At about 7pm that evening a group of nearly 1000 Guizers (men dressed in costumes) will gather, and half an hour later light their fire torches before collecting the longboat from the seafront in order to carry it in procession to King George V playing field whilst singing what is known as the Up Helly Aa song. At the field the boat is placed on the ground and the Guizers make a circle around it, waiting for the sound of a bugle. Once the last note dies away they all throw their lighted torches into the boat in order to set it on fire. As the boat burns they strike up another traditional Viking song, 'The Norseman's Home', which is sung until the boat lies as a burnt out smouldering ember.

But the burning of the Viking galleon is not the end of the day's activities. In groups, the Guizers commence a visitation of twelve public premises such as halls, schools and hotels which are purposefully opened to them. The Guizers move around from venue to venue, often taking all night to visit all twelve. At each location they will be greeted by hosts and guests and then be expected to perform some act, play or song. They will then complete a dance before moving on to the next location. This continues until the dawn of the next day, which thankfully is a public holiday in Lerwick. At least this allows everyone to recover from their exhaustion!

The Fire Festival of Lerwick is intended to celebrate the end of darkness and the rebirth of the sun. One day the Lord Jesus told a very important and religious man named Nicodemus that he needed to be born again. *"Except a man be born again, he cannot see the kingdom of God"* (John ch3v3). The Lord Jesus was saying that to enter Heaven we need to have a life given from Heaven which we only obtain when we turn from our sins and trust the Lord Jesus as our Saviour. The

Bible says, *"He that hath the Son hath life; and he that hath not the Son of God hath not life"* (1st John ch5v12). This is an event that's worth celebrating when you realize that God loves you and the Lord Jesus died to save you and you claim Him as your Saviour. *"For God so loved the world, that He gave His only begotten Son, that whosoever believeth in Him should not perish, but have everlasting life"* (John ch3v16).

A Burning Longboat

Liquid Gold

Did you ever play a game where you pretended to discover buried treasure? Maybe you have even dreamed of digging up something that was very valuable and had been hidden for hundreds of years. I guess we all have dreamed of doing something like this at one time or another.

In the 1970's, away out in the North Sea, researchers discovered large reserves of oil that were very valuable to the United Kingdom. There are many products which we make use of every day which are made from oil, including petrol and diesel to run cars and lorries, heating oil, fertilisers, plastics and even some fabrics. However, because this oil was right out in the middle of the North Sea there was much planning and work needed to build giant oil rigs on which men could work and live as they pumped this precious liquid from below the ocean's floor. Shetland was the closest part of the United Kingdom to this rare and exciting discovery and so it was chosen for the building of a giant oil terminal that could receive, treat, and process this oil when it came ashore. Ask anyone on mainland Britain about Shetland and invariably they will say something along the lines of "Oh, that's where the oil terminal is, at Sullom Voe." Yes, Sullom Voe is world famous because of its oil terminal!

Oil Rig

This terminal, covering a one thousand acre site at Calback Ness in North Mainland, was commenced in 1975 and was fully completed in 1981. Queen Elizabeth officially opened the facility on 9th May 1981. Sullom Voe is the largest oil and gas terminal in Europe, capable of processing more than one million barrels of oil a day, although it usually processes less than half of that now. That really is a lot of oil! It is also here at Sullom Voe that the huge supertankers will load North Sea oil in order to carry it all over the world. Due to its size and inaccessible location, Sullom Voe Oil Terminal has its own fire service on site, ready in case of emergency.

Thankfully, the terminal was built to make as small an impact on the islands as possible and visitors even tend to be impressed by the fact that it does not stand out like some ugly blot on the landscape. The gas stacks that rise high into the air from the site, burning off unwanted gas, look impressive in the dark. They can be seen from many places across North Mainland, ensuring that you always will know where Sullom Voe is. When the terminal was built, the old Scatsta World War Two airfield was renovated to provide a local airfield for the use of those working in this remote location.

The discovery of the oil fields in the North Sea brought much needed revenue into both the United Kingdom and the Shetland Islands. You will notice how well maintained and clean everything is here and also, perhaps, in what good order most of the roads are kept. Much of this has come about through the money which the discovery of oil has brought to the islands. In the Bible the psalmist said, "*I rejoice at Thy word, as one that findeth great spoil*" (Psalm 119v162). He was saying that He found the Bible, the Word of God, just as important as if he had made some discovery of great value. He also says in the same psalm, *"I love Thy commandments above gold; yea, above fine gold"* (Psalm 119v127). To the writer of this, the longest psalm in the Bible, the Word of God was more precious than the finest of gold. Do we appreciate and value our Bibles as this man did and are we prepared to discover the real treasures of God waiting to be found in its wonderful pages?

Babies, Birds and Brides

Shetland is full of stories, legends and incidents from the past which have been handed down from generation to generation. One of the most amazing must be the marvellous story of a rescue that took place on the island of Fetlar. To tell it we need to travel back in time about two hundred years.

On the island of Yell a young wife had given birth to a very small, prematurely born baby girl. It was harvest time and all the womenfolk were expected to work in the fields bringing in the harvest. It was a fine day and the young mother carried her baby, wrapped in a shawl, to the fields so that she could help with the work of harvesting. She placed her precious child on a corn rig and commenced to work alongside the other women. As time went on, the ladies moved further and further away from the baby until there was a considerable distance between mother and child. It was then that a huge sea eagle flew down and pounced on the sleeping baby, and despite the cries of alarm from the women carried the child off in its talons, flying over the sea to the island of Fetlar. Most of the women's husbands were out at sea, fishing, so the only ones available to mount a rescue were some of the older men who no longer went out to sea to fish. The only boat available that was not out at sea was in a very poor state of repair and hardly seaworthy. Into this the older men leapt and whilst some rowed hard, others bailed out the water that kept coming into the boat through its leaky hull. As these brave men sought to reach the island to which they had seen the eagle and baby fly, the women back on Yell knelt and prayed to God on the beach, asking Him to keep the baby safe.

Eventually, after great effort, the men arrived safely in Fetlar and upon finding a house asked a young twelve year old boy named Jimmy if he could direct them to the eagle's nest. This he agreed to do, and after observing the very poor state of the ropes the men had brought with them, decided that as he was the lightest he stood the best chance of being lowered down the cliff to the eagle's nest. Once above the nest site, high on the cliffs of Fetlar, the ropes were tested to ensure they could hold Jimmy's weight. As soon as the eagle and her mate saw Jimmy being lowered down the cliffs towards the nest containing not only the baby still wrapped in its shawl, but two young eaglets, they flew up with much noise and commenced to bombard him as he was carefully lowered down bit by bit, closer to the nest. Eventually Jimmy landed on the ledge where the nest was, and despite the continual attacks of the large birds and the young eaglets pecking at the baby's shawl, was able to pick up the little girl and place her safely in a bag his mother had given him. The men on the top lost no time in raising Jimmy and his precious cargo to the top of the cliffs where they, upon unwrapping the baby, found her none the worse for the awful ordeal she had gone through. The boat was speedily patched up by some of the men on Fetlar allowing a safer and more leisurely crossing back to Yell and the joyous reunion of the mother and her precious daughter.

But the story does not end there! Sixteen years later, Jimmy, who was now twenty-eight, whilst visiting Yell called in to see the family whose daughter he had rescued from certain death all those years before. As he ate and drank with her parents a most beautiful young lady came into the house, and for the first time she saw her strong, handsome, young saviour. This encounter commenced a courtship that in time led the rescuer and the rescued to embrace each other in marriage!

How wonderful is this story from the northern isles. And yet how greater in every way is the wonderful story of a Saviour's love, Who having come from Heaven brings rescue from the awful results of sin if we are prepared to trust Him, for the Bible says, *"The Father sent the Son to be the Saviour of the world"* (1st John ch4v14). Just like the little baby we were unable to do anything to save ourselves because the Bible says, *"Your iniquities have separated between you and your God, and your sins have hid His face from you, that He will not hear"* (Isaiah ch59v2). And yet the Lord Jesus came right to where He was needed in order to save us, lift us up from the danger of sin and then to allow us to live in Heaven with Him for all eternity. No wonder the apostle Paul says the Lord Jesus is *"the Son of God, Who loved me, and gave Himself for me"* (Galatians ch2v20).

Spectacular Shetland